Fernando de Faveri
Rafael Niebuhr Maia de Oliveira

Criminal analysis of homicides in Brusque in 2017

Fernando de Faveri
Rafael Niebuhr Maia de Oliveira

Criminal analysis of homicides in Brusque in 2017

Victim, accused and circumstances

ScienciaScripts

Imprint

Cover image: www.ingimage.com

This book is a translation from the original published under ISBN 978-613-9-68004-7.

Publisher:
Sciencia Scripts
is a trademark of
Dodo Books Indian Ocean Ltd. and OmniScriptum S.R.L publishing group

120 High Road, East Finchley, London, N2 9ED, United Kingdom
Str. Armeneasca 28/1, office 1, Chisinau MD-2012, Republic of Moldova, Europe
Printed at: see last page
ISBN: 978-620-8-19021-7

Summary

I. Introduction

The vast majority of homicide crimes involve the greatest amount of evidence production, due diligence, forensics, suspect and witness interviews, on the part of the public security agencies, especially the Civil Police.

In this sense, due to the complexity of ascertaining the authorship and materiality of this type of crime, various pieces of information, initially unknown, are ascertained and entered into police systems during investigations.

Based on this information, mainly that available in police investigations and their respective criminal proceedings, this statistical survey was carried out, extracting the most relevant characteristics of the crime, the accused and the victims.

Among the various areas of study in criminology, criminological profiling, in the words of Hamada[1] , can provide important indications in the search for social control and crime prevention. According to the author, initial profiling is done in order to help the police and the police authority to capture the individual. The initial profile is purely theoretical, based on theories and hypotheses based on pre-existing studies of subjects with the same characteristics. Based on the pre-existing characteristics common to these individuals, professionals in the field try to build a profile of the criminal in an attempt to predict their actions and thus prevent future delinquency through affirmative action in society.

However, in addition to providing important data for the application of sentences in specific cases, criminological profiling can do more by enabling the public authorities and civil society, by learning about the individual who occupies their prisons, to plan and promote public policies with the aim of preventing and avoiding criminal events.[2]

It is precisely in this context that this research is proposed, so that common traits among the individuals present in homicide crimes will be analyzed, both the accused and the victim, without any objective of contributing to their formation of guilt, but with the sole purpose of providing relevant data to understand the reality of **local violence** and, based on this, of crime in the region researched.

From time to time, the State Secretariat for Public Security publishes data on crime in Santa

---

1 HAMADA, Fernando Massami; Do Amaral, José Hamilton. **Criminal profiling as a criminological tool - encontro de iniciaçâo cientifica**. Vol. 4, 2009.

2 OLIVEIRA, Rafael Niebuhr Maia de; MARCOLLA, Fernanda Analu. Comparative analysis of the criminological profile of Brusque's prison population in relation to the national average: evidence of the selectivity of the Brazilian punitive system. In: OLDONI, Fabiano; SILVA, Pollyana Maria da (Orgs.). **Study on the prison system:** from selectivity to illegality. Joinville: Manuscritos Editora, 2017. p. 81-104.

Catarina on its website[3] , especially on crimes committed with violence or threat. However, the distinctive feature of this work lies in its typological detail (homicide) and specific geographical scope (Brusque).

In 2017, six (06) people were victims of homicide in the municipality of Brusque, of which five cases (83.3%) were solved by the police and only one remained unsolved.

The investigation is the responsibility of the Criminal Investigation Division (DIC), a specialized local unit responsible for investigating serious crimes, including homicide.[4]

It is noteworthy that, although the figures remain stable with slight fluctuations, in 2017 there was a slight increase in the number of homicides in the municipality since 2014. The statistical peak in this decade occurred in 2013, when ten people were victims of homicide in Brusque, as can be seen from the data provided by the Santa Catarina Public Security Secretariat and already widely reported in the press.[5]

The data analyzed here, referring to the year 2017, was extracted from the police investigations concluded and forwarded to the Judiciary, with the aim of better understanding the criminal phenomenon, which, ultimately, we believe will qualify future interventions in **public security.**

Added to this is the need for transparency in police agencies and their respective crime-solving rates, their internal studies to increase efficiency and their necessary accountability to society[6] and other supervisory bodies.

In order to do this, typological divisions were made of both the suspects and the victims, preserving their names, even when the crime received media coverage, considering that it was unnecessary to identify them for the purposes of this work, in addition to preserving their fundamental rights.

We also analyzed the circumstances of the crimes, their characteristics and elements, in an attempt to find out if there were any identifying elements, such as the time of day, the

3 For example: http://www.ssp.sc.gov.br/index.php/component/content/article/87-noticias/98- segurança-publica-divulga-dados-estatisticos-do-primeiro-semestre-de-2017.

4 In addition to homicide, the unit investigates the following offences: murder, drug trafficking, bank and cargo robbery, money laundering and crimes committed by criminal organizations. These duties are listed in Ordinance No. 0267/GAB/SSP/2017.

5 For example, a report in the newspaper O Municipio: https://omunicipio.com.br/brusgue- had-six-homicides-in-2017-highest-ever-recorded-since-2014/ Accessed on 10/04/2018.

6 Basically, it's about the necessary *accountability*, which, in our view, is nothing more than the duty of transparency of public bodies. For further reading, see Màrcio Adriano Anselmo: https://www.conjur.com.br/2016-dez-13/academia-policia-accountability-instrumento-eficiencia-policia-judiciaria. Accessed on 01/03/2018.

presence (or not) of narcotics, among other factors.

The criteria were based on the parameters of other similar studies already produced and published in the area, available on the internet[7] , differing from them once again because of the geographical delimitation, *in this case* restricted to the municipality of Brusque.

Similarly, with regard to the operational concept of those involved in the execution of the crimes, we opted for the term 'indicted', considering that, at the time of concluding the research, there had still been no definitive conviction of those involved, which is why this terminology was preferred to any other.

---

7 Cite, for example, the work of Airton José Ruschel, available at https://repositorio.ufsc.br/bitstream/handle/123456789/89042/232090. pdf?sequence=1. Accessed on 01/04/2018.

Chapter 1

This first chapter will present the information collected on the subjective characteristics of both the person responsible for the homicide and the victim, taking into account the geographical and temporal limitations proposed in this research.

Profile Characteristics

As a methodological choice, we will first present the personal characteristics of the accused, looking at their sex, age, color, education, marital status, profession, the relationship between the crime scene and their residence, as well as whether they knew their victim, and finally the probable motive for the crime and the naturalness of the accused.

Next, we will look at the victim's characteristics, focusing on gender, age, color, marital status, profession, the relationship between the crime scene and the victim's residence, their education, place of birth, and finally, whether there were any police records against them.

1.1 Profile of the accused

During the police phase, it is possible to accumulate the greatest amount of information about the person suspected of committing the murder. Although there is also the possibility of obtaining other elements in the procedural phase, there is no doubt that during the police investigation the characteristics of the profiles are shaped more clearly.

The data analyzed here was extracted exclusively from that reported in police reports and other information contained in police investigations, as well as that available in the Integrated Public Security System.

1.1.1 Sex of the accused and the victim

Table 1 - Sex of the accused and the victim

	Indicted	*Victim*
	Quantity	**Quantity**
Man	10	3
Woman	0	3
Total	**10**	**6**

Source: Integrated Public Security System - SISP

It should be noted that, in this specific case, we chose to insert the data of the victims next to the indictees, in order to facilitate visualization and statistical comparison.

As Table 1 shows, all those indicted in 2017 were male. As for the victims, only half of them were men (50%). An interesting counterpoint lies in the fact that, according to the 2010 census carried out by the Brazilian Institute of Geography and Statistics (IBGE), there are around 500,000 more women than men in Santa Catarina .[8]

In Brusque, specifically, another interesting piece of data, according to the same census, shows that the female population is 50.6%, therefore equally large.

The local data is in line with the reality throughout Brazil, in the sense that although women make up the majority of the population, they are not the perpetrators of homicide crimes. **In Brusque, according to the research, there were no women suspected or indicted of committing homicide**. However, as will be shown at the end of this research, one woman who had not been indicted was eventually denounced by the Public Prosecutor's Office.

1.1.2 Age of the accused

Table 2 - Age range of those indicted according to the IBGE scale

Age group	*Qty of indictees*
18 to 19 years old	**0**
20 to 24 years old	7
25 to 29 years old	**1**
30 to 34 years old	0
35 to 39 years old	**1**
40 to 44 years old	1
Total	**10**

Source: Integrated Public Security System - SISP

Table 2 gives us an idea of the age range of the majority of those involved in our research. The majority of them, seven (07), are between 20 and 24 years old (70%).

According to the 2010 census, around 5,616 men (5.3%) in Brusque are aged between 20 and 24[9] . This age group is also the one with the highest number of men in the municipality, representing a certain coherence when comparing these data proportionally.

Furthermore, one suspect is in the 25-29 age group (10%), another in the 35-39 age group (10%), and a final one in the 40-44 age group (10%).

This result is similar to the national average, since, according to a survey of the

8 http://dc.clicrbs.com.br/sc/noticia/2011/11/censo-2010-santa-catarina-tem-500-mil-mulheres-a-mais- than-men-3562973.html
9 https://censo2010.ibge.gov.br/sinopse/index.php?dados=26&uf=42

criminological profile made available by INFOPEN[10] regarding the distribution of the Brazilian prison population by age group, it can be seen that 55.07% of the national prison population is made up of young people - that is, people between the ages of 18 and 29:

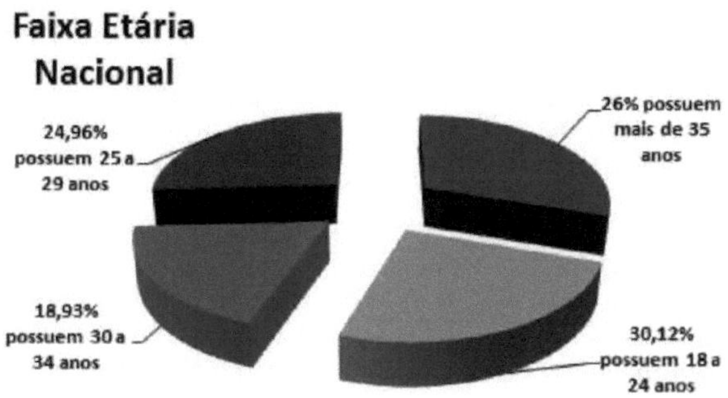

In this sense, it can be seen that in Brusque all the accused were over eighteen (18) years old at the time of the events, and there were no teenagers involved in any of the six murders perpetrated in 2017.

This situation, at least at a strictly local level, reveals a very important fact, because it contradicts common sense, which, when defending the reduction of the age of criminal responsibility, bases this claim on the argument of the rate of homicides committed by adolescents.

1.1.3 Color of the accused

Between 2012 and 2016, while the Brazilian population grew by 3.4% to 205.5 million, the number of people who declared themselves white fell by 1.8% to 90.9 million. The number of self-declared browns grew by 6.6% and blacks by 14.9%, reaching 95.9 million and 16.8 million, respectively. This is shown by the data on residents from the Continuous National Household Sample Survey 2016, released today by the IBGE .[11]

In the IBGE household surveys, the color of the residents is defined by self-declaration, i.e. the interviewee chooses one of the five options on the questionnaire: white, brown, black, yellow or indigenous .[12]

10INFOPEN, **Levantamento nacional de informaçôes Penitenciarias**, year 5, 2014. Available at: <http://dados.gov.br/dataset/infopen-levantamento-nacional-de-informacoes-penitenciarias> Accessed on: 27 jul. 2016.

11 https://agenciadenoticias.ibge.gov.br/agencia-noticias/2012-agencia-de-noticias/noticias/18282- pnad-c-moradores.html

12Ibid.

Thus, the data collected, reproduced below, was extracted as it was entered into the police and prison systems of Santa Catarina.

Table 3 - Color of suspect

	Quantity
White	**4**
Brown	3
Black	**2**
Not informed	1
Total	**10**

Source: Integrated Public Security System - SISP

Table 3 shows that the majority of those indicted are white (40%), three are brown (30%), two are black (20%) and one cannot be identified (10%), as there was no information about him in the systems searched.

On the national level, with regard to race, color or ethnicity, the information that stands out is the number of black or brown prisoners, who occupy 62.67% of the vacancies in the Brazilian prison system.[13]

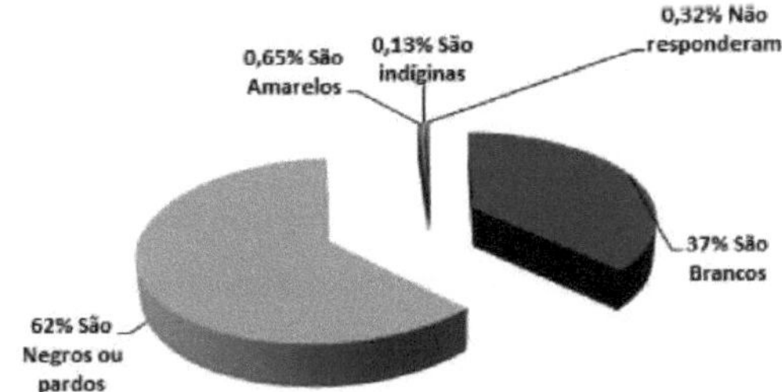

Racial proportion of people imprisoned in Brazil.

As far as the racial profile is concerned, the local panorama bears little resemblance to the national average, since while in Brusque white people account for 40% of those indicted for homicide, in Brazil the overall rate of prisoners with this characteristic is only 37%. It is believed that one of the relevant reasons for this situation is due to the colonization of the state, which is of European origin, thus influencing race.

13INFOPEN, **Levantamento nacional de informações Penitenciarias**, year 5, 2014. Available at: <http://dados.gov.br/dataset/infopen-levantamento-nacional-de-informacoes-penitenciarias> Accessed on: 27 jul. 2016.

In order to find out if the deviation was in line with the total number of whites by region, this data was sought from the 2010 IBGE census[14] , according to which 43.1% of the Brazilian population declared themselves to be brown and the highest percentage of this contingent was in the North (66.9%), with all regions showing percentages above 35%, except the South, with 16.5%. Also according to the census, 7.6% of those interviewed said they were black, and the highest percentage was in the Northeast (9.5%), with the Southeast (7.9%) following, while the South showed the lowest percentage (4.1%).

Distribution of the Brazilian population by region and color/race, 2010

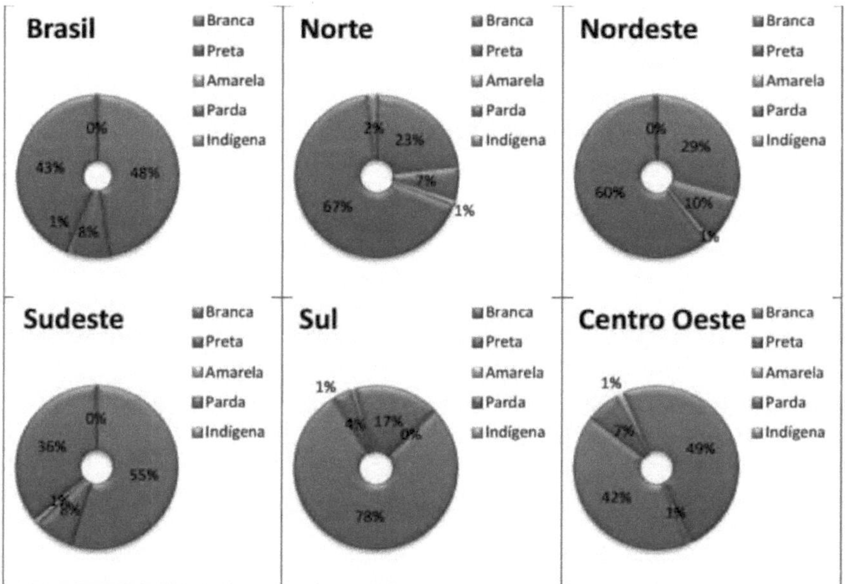

It can be seen that in the southern region the percentage of whites reaches 78%, while in the country as a whole this percentage is 48%. In other words, in the South there are approximately 60% more whites than the national average. This shows that the presence of whites involved in homicide crimes is not only influenced by the higher incidence of whites in this region, although it is clearly driven by this factor.

Finally, with regard to the racial issue, it can be seen that crime involving black people, whether in Brusque or nationally, is disproportionate to the presence of black people in the population. While in the south 18% of criminals declared themselves to be black or brown,

14 BRAZIL, Portal. **Study shows distribution of population by color or race.** Available at: <http://www.brasil.gov.br/cidadania-e-justica/2013/11/estudo-aponta-distribuicao-da-populacao-por- cor-ou-raca> Accessed on: October 28, 2016.

50% of those indicted also declared themselves to be so. Nationally, 67% of prisoners are black, while 49% of the general population is black .[15]

1.1.4 Education of the accused

The information collected on the level of education of the accused is not precise. When they are qualified in police systems, there are no options for detailing the series or type of course that qualified them, but only whether or not they completed a certain degree.

Table 4 - Schooling of the accused

	Quantity
1st grade incomplete	***1***
1st grade completed	*3*
2nd grade incomplete	***4***
2nd grade completed	*1*
Not informed	***1***
Total	10

Source: Integrated Public Security System - SISP

Looking at Table 4, if we group together those who have completed 1st grade and have not finished 2nd grade, we arrive at 70% of those involved. If we compare this data with the age range of the majority of those involved (20 to 24 years), we can see that the majority of those indicted are young and have little schooling, and none of them have higher education.

1.1.5 Marital status of the accused

The data entered into the police system are those provided by the accused himself when he is qualified in a given procedure, without the need for documentary proof, even though it is information that is easily understood and answered by the interrogated person at the time of his hearing.

Table 5 - Marital status of the accused

	Quantity
Single	**5**
Stable union	4
Married	**1**

15 OLIVEIRA, Rafael Niebuhr Maia de; MARCOLLA, Fernanda Analu. Comparative analysis of the criminological profile of the Brusque prison population in relation to the national average: evidence of the selectivity of the Brazilian punitive system. In: OLDONI, Fabiano; SILVA, Pollyana Maria da (Orgs.). **Study on the prison system:** from selectivity to illegality. Joinville: Manuscritos Editora, 2017. p. 81-104.

Total	10

Source: Integrated Public Security System - SISP

Table 5 shows that 50% of those indicted are single and 40% have a relationship that is considered stable. Another interesting fact is that only one of the defendants is or was married, which may suggest that a solid family background can contribute to reducing the vulnerability of those eventually involved in violent crime.

In this sense, Calhau[16] (2005) cites the importance of the family in effectively controlling this problem, as well as highlighting some of the consequences when there are flaws in the family structure:

The family is a fundamental part of this intricate problem. An unstructured family can produce adults who have problems coping with the complexity of social life, bringing them closer to drugs and unbridled alcoholism, which provides opportunities to commit crimes. In this context, the effective application of the child and adolescent protection rules of Federal Law 8069/90, with the support of psychologists, social workers and other professionals, would prevent many adolescents from later opting for the path of crime.

Obviously, any conclusions on the subject of family structure and violence in the Brusque context would require specific research on the subject, which is beyond the scope of this work.

1.1.6 Profession of the accused

The "profession" data was also extracted from the information provided by the suspect during the qualification process at the police station, using the most recent data.

However, it is possible that there may be a subsequent statement from the employer, a copy of the work permit or some other document proving the defendant's situation, attached to the criminal action, which could contradict the data presented below.

Table 6 - Occupation of the accused

	Quantity
Unemployed	**2**
Metalworker	*1*
Driver	***1***
Painter	*1*
Bricklayer	**4**
Taxi driver	1

16 CALHAU, Lélio Braga. **Social control - Informal and Formal.** Available at:http://clodomiro.xpg.uol.com.br/e724.html. Accessed on: Aug. 11, 2016.

Total	**10**

Source: Integrated Public Security System - SISP

An analysis of the data extracted from the system shows that almost half of those indicted qualified as bricklayers (40%). The second highest percentage is unemployed, with 20%.

The survey also included taxi drivers, painters, drivers and metalworkers, all of whom were employed by one of the accused, respectively.

It can be seen that the professions reported require low levels of schooling, half of them linked to construction (bricklayer and painter), data consistent with that shown in table 4.

In addition, the majority of those involved who had a job were engaged in precarious working relationships, characterized by their volatility in time (in relation to the period of time they are working), service provider (which changes very frequently), which generate insecurity in relation to the workers' monthly income, which hampers their personal and family planning.

Furthermore, it has not been possible to ascertain or qualify the economic situation of each of those involved, and it is hasty to point out their incomes, based only on the profession mentioned, despite indications that the majority have low incomes.

1.1.7 Place of the crime and residence of the accused

According to 2016 IBGE census data, Brusque has just over 125,000 inhabitants and an approximate area of 283.223 km^2 . It also has around 33 neighbourhoods in its territorial area, whether or not they have been regularized by law .[17]

Table 7 - Crime scene

Neighborhood	*Number of victims*
Limeira	***2***
Limoeiro	*1*
Nova Brasilia	***1***
Saint Lucia	*1*
Zantao	***1***

Source: Integrated Public Security System - SISP

With the exception of the Limeira neighborhood, where two of the six murders occurred in 2017, there was a randomness in the occurrence of the other crimes in the regions of the municipality.

Another interesting fact is that none of the murders occurred in Brusque's five most populous

17 https://cidades.ibge.gov.br/brasil/sc/brusque/panorama

neighborhoods.

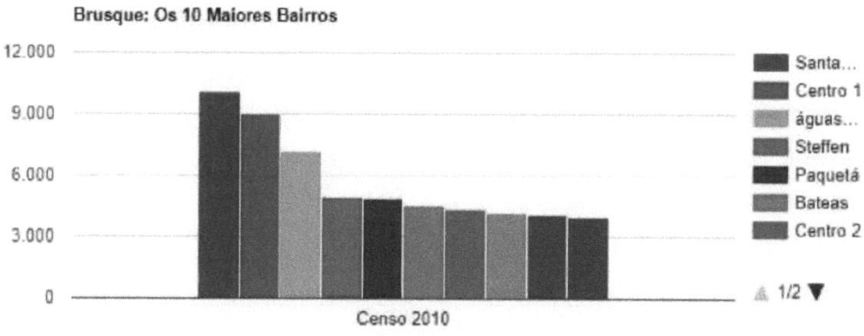

Fonte: http://populacao.net.br/os-maiores-bairros-brusque_sc.html

Furthermore, not all of the accused lived in the same neighborhood where they committed the murder. The 10 indicted, according to the data he declared in the police records, lived in different neighborhoods of the municipality, as will be seen below.

Table 8 - Residence of the accused

Neighborhoods	***Qty of indictees***
Bateas	1
Maluche Garden	**1**
Limeira	2
Limoeiro	**1**
Nova Brasilia	1
Deep Well	**1**
Saint Lucia	1
Zantao	**2**

Source: Integrated Public Security System - SISP

Of the two victims from the Limeira neighborhood, their respective tormentors, 20% of those indicted, also lived in the same neighborhood. The victim from the Bateas neighborhood also had her tormentor living in the same place. The other crime scenes (50%) did not necessarily correlate with where the accused lived.

1.1.8 Did the accused know his victim?

Knowing the possible relationship between the perpetrator and the victim is extremely important for the conduct of the police investigation and for the trial during the procedural phase, as it is one of the points from which the motivation for the crime is drawn.

Almost all of the homicide cases in Brusque involve people who knew their victims beforehand, as police reports show.

<u>**Graph 1**</u>

Did the accused know his victim?

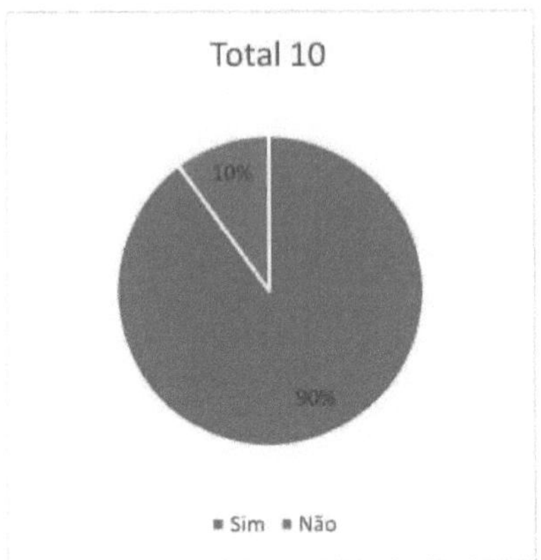

Considering the elements of the investigations, 9 of the 10 indictees knew their victims. Only one, who was indicted as a participant in the crime of murder, could not prove in the reports that he had previously known his victim.

On the other hand, five of the six victims also knew their executioners. In the only crime that wasn't solved, it wasn't possible to ascertain whether or not the victim knew in advance who had taken his life.

1.1.9 Motive for the crime

The data on the motives for the crime was extracted from the indictment reports made by the police chief at the end of the investigation, as well as other elements that may have been included in the inquiries. Although the motives may have other outcomes during the procedural phase, the data analyzed here is limited to that collected during the police phase.

Table 9 - Motivation for the crime

Reason	***Quantity***
Jealousy	1
Commercial disagreement	**1**
Unknown	1

Drug debt	1
Revenge	2

Source: Integrated Public Security System (Sistema Integrado de Segurança Pùblica - SISP) and indictment reports from the Criminal Investigation Division (Divisâo de Investigaçâo Criminal - DIC) of the Brusque district.

In order to facilitate the analysis and understanding of the data, the table above has been drawn up according to the type and circumstances that the police reports took into account in the elucidation of the case, as well as the evidence and statements taken at the police stage.

Of the six murders, one (16.6%) occurred because of jealousy, when the husband killed his wife after an argument at a party they had attended, in a typical case of femicide .[18]

We had another (16.6%) homicide in which the victim sold a motorcycle to his tormentors, who, after failing to make the agreed payment, were confronted by the victim, who ended up being murdered for repossessing the property they had bought and not paid for.

Two other victims were murdered after making threats and allegedly stealing property from the home of one of the accused, who, after becoming aware of the facts, together with a third party, also included in the statistics, went looking for the victims, found them and killed them.

There was also the emblematic case of the young woman who was beaten and burned alive because of debts with drug dealers and alleged love affairs with an accused involved in criminal factions.

Finally, in the only unsolved case, it was not possible to clearly identify the real motivation that led to the murder of the victim.

1.1.10 Place of birth of the accused

The data relating to the defendant's place of birth are those provided by the documents they were carrying when the procedure was carried out at the police station or when they were arrested for some reason.

Furthermore, when any of them makes their general identity record in the state of Santa Catarina, through the General Institute of Forensics - IGP, all their data, including their place

18 The crime of intimate femicide has been provided for in legislation since the entry into force of Law No. 13.104/2015, which amended art. 121 of the Penal Code (Decree-Law No. 2.848/1940) to provide for femicide as a qualifying circumstance of the crime of murder. Thus, the murder of a woman committed for reasons of her female sex, i.e. when the crime involves: "domestic and family violence and/or contempt for or discrimination against the condition of women". Available at: "http://www.agenciapatriciagalvao.org.br/dossies/violencia/violencias/feminicidio/"

of birth, is shared in the Integrated Public Security System - SISP.

Table 10 - Place of birth of the accused

City/State	*Quantity*
Buerarema/BA	2
Brusque/SC	**1**
Clevelândia/PR	1
Curitiba/PR	**1**
Dionisio Cerqueira/SC	1
Foz do Iguaçu/PR	**1**
Lages/SC	1
Palmas/PR	**1**
Pitanga/PR	1

Source: Integrated Public Security System - SISP

Table 10 gives us an idea of the place of birth of those indicted in Brusque. One relevant fact is that only one of them was born in the municipality of Brusque.

Another fact is that half of those indicted (50%) are from the state of Paranà. Another two are from the same town in Bahia, Buerarema. The remaining 30% are from other regions of the state of Santa Catarina, which are not even close to the municipality where they committed the crime.

These figures may indicate a change in the criminological profile of criminals in the city of Brusque. This is because they show significant distortions when compared with the results obtained in a survey carried out with inmates at the Brusque Prison Unit in 2016, when the following result was obtained, as published at the time:

> In order to understand the local reality, we asked the inmates about their city and state of origin, and found that 37% are from Brusque, 33% from other cities in Santa Catarina, 14% from the state of Paranà, 7% from Rio Grande do Sul, and only 5% from the Northeast and 3% from the state of São Paulo. This means that 70% of the inmates at the Brusque UPA come from the state of Santa Catarina .[19]

---

19 OLIVEIRA, Rafael Niebuhr Maia de; MARCOLLA, Fernanda Analu. Comparative analysis of the criminological profile of the Brusque prison population in relation to the national average: evidence of the selectivity of the Brazilian punitive system. In: OLDONI, Fabiano; SILVA, Pollyana Maria da (Orgs.). **Study on the prison system:** from selectivity to illegality. Joinville: Manuscritos Editora, 2017. p. 81-104.

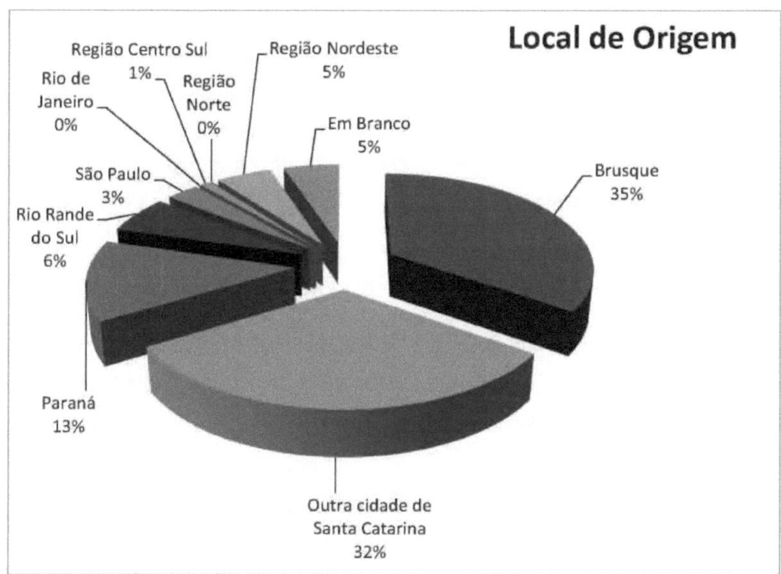

One of three conclusions can be drawn from this: either the criminological profile has been changing in recent years, or criminals from outside the state of Santa Catarina, although they form a minority of the prison population as a whole, are more prevalent in relation to capital crimes. There is also the possibility that the profile in the period surveyed is merely circumstantial, depending on the continuation of the study in the coming years to show trends in one direction or another.

1.2 Victim profile

Although it is recognized that in police and procedural practice more importance is given to the data of the perpetrators, since they are the ones investigated, tried and convicted, it is equally important to trace the profile of the victims, seeking to study and understand them.

This is because the victim plays a fundamental role in the structure of the crime, since, with the study of victimology, we know its importance in the analysis of crime, since its information is fundamental for clarifying crimes, such as those committed in hiding, with violence or serious threat, without which it would be impossible to gather clear and real information.[20]

20PAULA, Tania Braga de. **Criminology: study of the sociological schools of crime and the practice of criminal offenses.** 2013. 47 f. Monograph (Graduation in Law) - Centro Universitàrio do Norte Paulista - UNORP, Sao José do Rio Preto, 2013. P. 16

1.2.1 Sex of the victim

Table 11 - Sex of victims

Man	*Woman*
3	***3***

Source: Integrated Public Security System - SISP

Table 11 shows that half of the victims were men and half were women. Table 1 also shows that the female population in Brusque is slightly larger than the male population.

In comparative and proportional terms, in 2017 the gender of the victims kept pace with the municipality's demographic census. On the other hand, this is not the case in terms of national statistics, as determined by the IBGE in the 2010 census.

Because of violence, for every woman between the ages of 20 and 24 who dies in Brazil, the country loses four men in the same age group. In Alagoas, top of the ranking, eight men die in this age group for every woman .[21]

This survey recorded a total of 1,034,418 deaths in the country from August 2009 to July 2010. There were 133.4 male deaths for every 100 female deaths. However, it is in the 15 to 19, 20 to 24 and 25 to 29 age groups that the number of male deaths is much higher. In the 20 to 24 age group, 80.8% of those who die are men .[22]

In this sense, it can be seen that in 2017, Brusque was in line with the national averages indicated in the aforementioned census. Although the number of homicides was significantly low, it is still possible to compare that there was a significant proportion (50%) of murders of women in our municipality.

1.2.2 Victim's age

Table 12 - Age range of victims according to IBGE

Age group	***Quantity***
18 to 19 years old	***2***
20 to 24 years old	***0***
25 to 29 years old	***0***
30 to 34 years old	***1***
35 to 39 years old	***2***

21https://oglobo.globo.com/brasil/dados-do-ibge-confirmam-que-violencia-mata-mais-homens-jovens-3256278
22 Ibid

40 to 44 years old	***0***
45 to 49 years old	***1***

Source: Integrated Public Security System - SISP

The ages of the victims were established at the time the crime took place. Looking at table 12, it can be seen that the age range of the victims was very diverse, with no clustering, even grouping, in any particular age group.

Around 33.3% of the victims were aged 18 or 19 when they were murdered. If these are grouped together with the perpetrators, who were under 25, the figure rises to 75%, showing that the ratio of accused to victims is mostly young.

The other victims were aged over 30 and under 50, with no statistical correlation in this age group, probably consisting of circumstantial elements.

1.2.3 Victim's color

The color of the victim was ascertained, as well as that of the accused, from the information in the police systems, or by analyzing the existing photograph of the victim when this information was not described in the database.

Table 13 - Color of victim

	Quantity
White	***4***
Brown	***1***
Not informed	***1***
Total	***6***

Source: Integrated Public Security System - SISP

As table 13 shows, the vast majority of victims were white (66.6%), with only one brown victim and no black victims. As table 3 also shows, in which the majority of those indicted are also white, the victims are no different.

In addition, as I mentioned at the time, Brusque's population has a large number of white residents, in proportion to brown and black residents. Following this statistical proportion, perpetrators and victims reflect the characteristics of the local population itself.

1.2.4 Marital status of the victim

Like the marital status of the accused, the information of this nature found in police databases is that provided by the victim themselves when they go to the police station for any procedure.

Table 14 - Marital status of the victim

	Quantity
Single	***3***
Married	3
Total	**6**

Source: Integrated Public Security System - SISP

Considering the data above, half of the victims were single and the other half were married. It should be noted, however, that this information was not checked in public records or in any other body, but only the information passed on by the victims, in good faith, in police databases.

1.2.5 Victim's profession

Table 15 - Victim's profession

Quantity	
Unemployed	***2***
Student	*1*
Driver	***1***
Not informed	*1*
Weaver	***1***
Total	*6*

Source: Integrated Public Security System - SISP

These professions were extracted according to the statements of the victims or third parties, also when they went to the police station for some procedure.

In this sense, and analyzing the data above, one third of the victims were unemployed. On the other hand, at least half of them (50%), even if there is no information, were doing some kind of work/occupational activity at the time of the crime.

Furthermore, it is not possible to identify any correlation between the professional data and the homicide rate in the municipality, since, even if we understand the possibility of a possible connection, the number of murders, despite a slight increase in 2017, is still far below the national average.

1.2.6 Crime scene and victim's home

At this point, we analyzed whether the victims lived in the same neighborhood where they were murdered. This analysis aims to identify whether there is any correlation between the victim's residence and the place where the crimes took place.

Table 16 - Residence of the victims

Neighborhoods	*Number of victims*
Lajeado Baixo/ Guabiruba	*1*
Limeira	***2***
Limoeiro	*1*
Saint Lucia	***1***
Zantao	*1*
Total	***6***

Source: Integrated Public Security System - SISP

Looking at table 16, it can be seen that, with the exception of the Limeira neighborhood, where two victims lived, there was a proportional division of the others among the various neighborhoods in the region.

Another interesting fact is that if you look at table 15 together with table 7, which deals with crime locations, only one of the victims wasn't murdered in the exact same neighborhood where he lived.

The victim who was murdered in the Nova Brasilia neighborhood was the only one who didn't live there. All the others were killed at or near home or at their place of work.

This data, at least in theory, could indicate that the murders in Brusque in 2017 were premeditated, since the statistics don't show that the victims were murdered in random places in the city, or that they were concentrated in a certain region of the municipality, such as conflicts between drug dealers, gang wars or similar issues.

1.2.7 Victim's schooling

As well as the data extracted about the accused, the victim's education level is that declared when the case was registered at the police station.

Table 17 - Victim's schooling

	Quantity
Literate	*1*
1st grade incomplete	**3**
I^0 complete degree	1
2nd grade incomplete	**1**
Total	6

Source: Integrated Public Security System - SISP

In table 17, there is also no precise information on how many grades the victim had. This is because the police system itself restricts itself, when qualifying schooling, to what level the person has completed and whether it is complete or incomplete.

One point to note is that 100% of the victims did not complete high school, and half of them didn't even complete first grade. None of them stand out from the others, with some higher education or no literacy. There is a small pattern among them.

1.2.8 Place of birth of the victim

Table 18 - Place of birth of the victim

City/State	*Quantity*
Brusque/SC	*4*
Indaial/SC	***1***
Paranaguâ/PR	*1*
Total	***6***

Source: Integrated Public Security System - SISP

Table 18 shows that the majority of victims were from Brusque (66.6%). If we add the victim from Indaial/SC, 83.3% of the victims in our municipality are from the state of Santa Catarina.

The exception is just one victim from the city of Paranaguà/PR. This data contrasts with table 10, in which 50% of those indicted are from that state, and 16.6% of the victims, that is, only one of them, is from the state of Paranà.

On the other hand, only one of the perpetrators was born in Brusque, as shown in table 10, and the vast majority of the victims (4) were also born in the city where they were murdered.

1.2.9 Victims' police records

The typologies used are those contained in the database made available at the time the police officer, the system operator, qualifies the conduct of the person presented at the police station, for some crime or other reason.

Table 19 - Victims' backgrounds

Passage	*Quantity*
Threat against man	1
Threats against women	**1**
Theft	2
Forgery of a seal or public sign	**1**

Bodily injury	3
Woman bodily injury (violence home)	**1**
Possession of drugs	1
No history	**2**

Source: Integrated Public Security System - SISP

Table 19 shows that four of the six victims had a police record at some point in their lives, either as the perpetrator or as a suspect under investigation.

It should also be noted that this data is restricted to the data held in the Santa Catarina databases, and it is not known whether any of them had a police record in any other state of the federation.

Another point worth highlighting is that only two of the victims had no police record. Proportionally speaking, this data may show that most of the victims were, or at least had been, involved in the practice of illicit conduct, which may have contributed to the motivation for some of their murders.

Chapter 2

Homicide Processing Profile

In addition to the subjective analysis of the subjects involved in homicide crimes, analyzing each objective characteristic of the homicides perpetrated in Brusque in 2017 can help to verify whether or not there is any pattern in the way they occurred, such as the demographic region, the time of day, the type of weapon used, the relationship between the victim and their tormentor, among other characteristics.

2.1 Characteristics of intentional homicide

The following will look at the characteristics of the six murders that took place in 2017, as well as data on the accused, the victims and other relevant characteristics that may reveal a pattern between them.

2.1.1 Crime Day Shift

The time at which the murders took place may be of fundamental importance when it comes to establishing a pattern in which murderers plan to execute their victims.

In order to standardize the shifts in which they occurred, the morning shift was separated as the period from 6:01 am to 12:00 pm, the afternoon shift from 12:01 pm to 6:00 pm and the night shift from 6:01 pm to 6:00 am.

Table 20 - Shift on the day of the crime

Shift	*Qty of indictees*
Morning	**3**
Afternoon	0
Night	**7**
Total	10

Source: Integrated Public Security System - SISP

Table 20 shows that the majority of those indicted (70%) committed their murders during the night shift. This data reveals, at least in theory, a certain pattern as to the preferred time for the criminal intent.

The remaining 30% of indictees murdered their victim during the morning shift. They were the exception to the rest.

Another fact worth noting is that none of the cases occurred in the afternoon, believing that during this period, in broad daylight and with reasonable human movement, it is more fearful of carrying out the crime due to the increased chance of capture.

2.1.2 Crime scene and place of death

Table 21 - Crime scene and victim's place of death

Location	*Number of victims*
Home	*2*
Work	*1*
Via Publica	*3*

Source: Integrated Public Security System - SISP

According to table 21, all the victims died at the scene, and none of them were found alive or died on the way to or in hospital.

Except for one case, in which the victim was killed at home, but ended up being transported to the public highway, where they were found. In all the other cases, the victims were found where they were murdered.

2.1.3 Weapon used in the crime

In the police reports analyzed, the manner in which the victim was murdered was determined, as well as the means or weapon used by the perpetrators at the time of the crime.

Table 22 - Weapon of crime

Weapon/Means	*Quantity*
Strangulation	*1*
Burns	***1***
.380 caliber pistol	*1*
.32 caliber revolver	***2***
Homemade firearm	*1*

Source: Integrated Public Security System - SISP

Table 22 shows that 66.6% of homicides involved the use of a firearm. Evaluating the use of firearms can give a statistical idea of the most common means used to commit homicide in Brusque.

As in most of the country, the firearm is still the most commonly used means of murder, and the reason is obvious: it is the tool with the highest lethality rate if used with a certain amount of skill .[23]

In the other cases analyzed, there was one death by strangulation, which took place in the victim's own home. Finally, and most cruelly, there was a death by burning, where the victim, after being beaten by his tormentors, was set on fire alive.

2.1.4 Type of crime scene and type of relationship

The relationship between the victim and the accused was analyzed according to the police reports signed by the police chief, when the relationship between the parties was more clearly ascertained.

Table 23 - Place of crime and type of relationship

Relationships	Via Publica	Home	Work
Loving	0	1	0
Unknown	3	0	0
Trade agreement	0	3	0
Drug trafficking	3	0	0
Total	6	4	0

Source: Integrated Public Security System (Sistema Integrado de Segurança Pùblica - SISP) and indictment reports from the Criminal Investigation Division (Divisao de Investigagao Criminal - DIC) of the Brusque/SC district.

The correlation between the place of the crime and the type of relationship was made between the accused, whether or not they knew their victim and the type of relationship they had, as well as where they actually committed their crimes.

Table 23 shows that only 30% of those indicted had no previous relationship with their victims, which is why they were classified in the unknown column.

Another 30% of the suspects murdered their victim in her own home, and their relationship involved a business transaction, which later led to a disagreement between the parties and the consequent death of one of them.

A further 30% of those indicted carried out their criminal intent because they were in debt for drug trafficking. They also knew their victim beforehand.

Those who carried out the crime on the basis of a relationship through drug trafficking, and those who had no previous relationship with the victims, if added together, represent 60%

23 http://agenciabrasil.ebc.com.br/geral/noticia/2017-06/sete-em-cada-dez-homicidios-no-brasil-foram- with-firearms-in-2015

of the indictees who murdered on public roads, which represents half of the murders in this type of location.

Finally, there is a column referring to the crime scene "Work", which was not filled in because it was the only murder in which it was not possible to determine the perpetrator. It is therefore impossible to determine the type of relationship between the victim and his executioner.

2.1.5 Presence of drugs in crime

The presence of drugs in homicides can reflect whether or not this is the main reason for homicidal intent. One example is the capital Florianopolis, where in 2017 there was a 92% increase in the number of violent deaths .[24]

This increase was apparently due to the territorial dispute over the command of drug trafficking in the region, between the criminal factions that have been taking over territory there year after year, according to the authors' observation of the day-to-day work of the Judicial Police, which has been widely publicized in the media.

In the specific case of Brusque, where the number of violent deaths was infinitely lower than in the state capital, we analyzed the presence or absence of drug involvement in homicides, based on police reports and police reports on the case.

Table 24 - Presence of drugs in crime

YesNo
15

Source: Integrated Public Security System (Sistema Integrado de Segurança Pùblica - SISP) and indictment reports from the Criminal Investigation Division (Divisâo de Investigaçâo Criminal - DIC) of the Brusque/SC district.

Initially, it is worth noting that of the data analyzed, in only one (01) case was it clear that the crime occurred because of explicit involvement in drug trafficking. It is also worth mentioning that this was the only victim who had a police record for possession of narcotics.

One of the murders, it must be said, remained unsolved, and there was no information during the investigation that the victim was involved in drug trafficking, nor was any presence of drugs detected at the scene of the crime.

Another murder took place simply because of jealousy and another because of a business disagreement involving the sale of a motorcycle. Finally, the other two murders, which took

24 https://ndonline.com.br/florianopolis/noticias/florianopolis-encerra-2017-com-recorde-historico-de-violent deaths

place against a couple living in the Limeira neighborhood, have no concrete information about the relationship between crime and drug trafficking, but cannot be ruled out.

This is because, although the couple may have had some involvement in drug trafficking or drug use, an analysis of the police reports shows that they were killed in revenge for one of their tormentors, who allegedly had his house previously invaded by the victims and robbed.

2.1.6 Type of police record of the accused

As with the item on the victim's background, the textual typologies available in police databases were also used here.

The analysis of the data seeks to ascertain whether or not the accused had a certain inclination to commit criminal conduct, violent or not, for those who believe in such a possibility, or whether they committed their crimes on a one-off basis.

Table 25 - Police records of the accused

Police record	***Qty of indictees***
Tampering with vehicle identification markings	*1*
An infraction analogous to the crime of theft	***1***
Forgery of a seal or public sign	*1*
Counterfeit currency	***2***
Illegal possession of a permitted firearm	*2*
Possession of drugs	***4***
Reception	*2*
Theft	***2***
Domestic Violence (Threats)	*2*
Domestic Violence (injury to a woman)	***3***
Drug trafficking	*4*
No history	***2***

Source: Integrated Public Security System - SISP

Looking at table 25, there is a considerable range of police passages for the accused, bearing in mind that 80% of them had them. Only two perpetrators had no criminal record.

The two most recurrent police records are possession for personal consumption and drug trafficking, with four (04) suspects involved in each of these, with two (02) cases involving the same individual.

In third place is bodily injury against women, which occurred in the context of domestic violence, with 3 (three) indictees with such tickets. It is also noteworthy that, at least in Santa

Catarina, none of them had previously been convicted of homicide.

In addition, the range of tickets was very diverse, with two defendants with tickets for illegal possession of a firearm and two defendants with tickets for robbery also standing out.

On the other hand, the data revealed that the majority of those indicted were already involved in the practice of illegal conduct, the exception being only two (02) who had no previous record until they killed their victims.

Therefore, it can be seen that the crime of homicide in Brusque in 2017, even if it is not mostly related to a dispute between drug dealers, considering the diversity of causes and victims statistically documented, one cannot exclude the four (04) drug trafficking tickets and, likewise, another four (04) for drug use, in a universe of 10 perpetrators, which represents 40% of the population surveyed, if the data is not aggregated.

Chapter 3

Result of the court case

At this point in the research, we addressed the sequence, in the judicial sphere, of the procedures for ascertaining the authorship, materiality and culpability of the indictees identified. Such an investigation can provide data on the assertiveness of the determination of guilt in the police phase, as well as the qualified collection of evidence of the elements necessary to hold the guilty parties accountable.

To this end, a brief summary of each of the cases up to the closing date of this research, May 20, 2018, will be presented, with a final report on the conclusions that could be drawn from these results when compiled.

3.1 *Court Case No. 0001239-70.2017.8.24.0011*

In this first case analyzed, the crime occurred on January 8, 2017, as recorded in Police Report 531-2017-4. The investigation was concluded on April 18, 2017, and two (02) people were indicted.

The Public Prosecutor's Office, in turn, denounced the exact people indicted by the Police Delegate on May 5, 2017, which was received by the judge on May 11, 2017.

When they were duly summoned, both men presented a preliminary defense through the same lawyer, who alleged preliminary objections, which were rejected by the judge, and failed to comment on the merits of the complaint at that time. There is no evidence in the case file of any habeas corpus proceedings against any decision handed down in the case file.

The hearing was held on the date initially designated (29/11/2017), and a deadline was set for the parties to present their closing arguments, which was complied with by the prosecution and, finally, by the defense, on February 22, 2018.

Since then, the case has been awaiting sentencing.

3.2 *Court Case No. 0003952-18.2017.8.24.0011*

In this case, the crime took place on May 18, 2017, as recorded in police report 531-2017-62. The investigation was concluded on September 22, 2017, with one (01) person indicted.

The Public Prosecutor's Office, in turn, denounced the exact person indicted by the Police Delegate on October 4, 2017, which was received by the judge on October 13, 2017, decreeing the preventive detention of the same, as requested by the "Parquet", upon recommendation of the Police Delegate.

Duly summoned, he presented a preliminary defense through a constituted defender, who did not allege any preliminary objections to the merits of the case, failing to comment on the merits of the complaint at that time. There is no news in the case file of any habeas corpus proceedings against any decision handed down in the case file.

The hearing was not completed on the date initially set (29/11/2017), due to the absence of prosecution witnesses, but at the insistence of the prosecutor, a new date was set (06/12/2017) for their hearing.

On the appointed date, the second hearing was held, and the investigation was concluded, with final oral arguments being presented, which led to the case file being concluded for sentencing on the same date.

A day later, on December 7, 2017, the judge pronounced the defendant guilty, as requested in the indictment, denying him the right to appeal in freedom. An appeal in the strict sense of the word was filed against this sentence, in which the exclusion of the qualifiers of the crime of homicide was requested, with the defense acquiescing to the materiality and authorship of the crime of simple homicide.

The Public Prosecutor of the State of Santa Catarina expressed his opinion that the appeal should be allowed. In an analysis of the appeal, the Court ruled that it should not be heard. Once this decision had become final, the judge summoned the defense to call the witnesses it wished to hear in plenary, an order that is awaiting compliance.

3.3 Court Case No. 0002182-87.2017.8.24.0011

In this case, the crime took place on May 21, 2017, as recorded in police report 531-2017-64. The investigation was concluded on June 6, 2017, with one (01) person indicted.

The Public Prosecutor's Office denounced the exact person indicted by the Police Delegate on June 23, 2017, which was received by the judge on June 28, 2017.

Duly summoned, he presented a preliminary defense through a constituted defender on November 6, 2017, in which he did not allege preliminary objections to the merits of the case, failing to comment on the merits of the complaint at that time. There is no news in the case file of any habeas corpus proceedings against any decision handed down in the case file.

The hearing took place on the date initially set (02/07/2018), with the Public Prosecutor's

Office presenting oral closing arguments. The defense was given 3 days to present closing arguments by memorials.

On March 1, 2018, a sentence was passed in which the judge pronounced the defendant, as requested in the indictment, granting him the right to appeal in freedom. An appeal in the strict sense of the word was filed against this sentence by a lawyer, who pleaded for the defendant's imprisonment on the grounds of self-defense of honor, or at least for all the qualifiers to be excluded, which in his view were not proven.

Once the appeal was received, the Public Prosecutor's Office was summoned to file counter-appeals, which as of the end of this research has not yet occurred.

3.4 Lawsuit No. 0000845-29.2018.8.24.0011

In this case, the crime took place on May 12, 2017, as recorded in police report 34-2017-64345, which initially classified the event as "disappearance of a person". The investigation, after some preventive and temporary arrests, as well as representations to break telephone secrecy, was concluded on July 6, 2017, indicating three (03) people as the main agents and one (01) person as a participant.

On July 14, 2017, the Public Prosecutor's Office decided to indict the three people indicted by the police chief as the main perpetrators of the crime. However, as for the participants, in addition to the person indicted, it included another person, a female, whose guilt had been ruled out by the police chief.

The complaint was received on July 18, 2017. One of the participants, who was summoned, requested to be admitted to the proceedings by a lawyer, who subsequently waived the powers granted to him.

In the absence of a defense within the legal time limit, the judge appointed lawyers to act as proxy defenders.

Subsequently, on August 21, 2017, the first defendant presented his defense, in which he did not allege preliminary objections on the merits, failing to comment on the merits of the complaint at that time.

The following day, the second defendant filed a preliminary objection to the complaint's inapplicability, and left to present his defense on the merits at the end of the trial.

On August 24, the third defendant presented his defense, in which, unlike the others, he requested the defendant's summary acquittal, as well as presenting his assessments on the merits of the complaint.

The preliminary arguments were rejected by the magistrate, without any habeas corpus being filed against this decision. As for the defendant included in the indictment by the Public Prosecutor's Office, because she is in an unknown and undisclosed location, it was decided to drop the case against her on September 21, 2017. There is no news in the case file of any habeas corpus proceedings against any decision handed down in the case file.

The case file shows great difficulty in locating witnesses, which probably delayed the date of the hearing, which took place on October 25, 2017, in which the investigation was completed, with a three-day deadline for the prosecution and defense to present closing arguments.

In a sentence handed down on November 24, 2017, all the defendants were sentenced by the judge, who also denied them the right to appeal in freedom.

On December 7, 2017, the court was informed of the death of the defendant, who was in an unknown place and in relation to whom the case had been split. Subsequently, the case file was informed that this defendant had died, which led to the termination of the proceedings against her.

In December 2017, two of the appointed defenders lodged appeals in the strict sense of the word, which, after being received by the "a quo" judge, were partially upheld in relation to the Defendant Charles, in order to rule out the qualification of ulterior motive, while the appeal of the Defendant Robson was not heard.

Robson was convicted of both the crime of murder and the crime of concealing a corpse, while Charles was cleared of both charges. The Public Prosecutor's Office filed an appeal against this decision, seeking to have the jury annulled. The appeal is awaiting counter-appeals from the defense and will then go before the Santa Catarina Court of Justice.

With regard to the two defendants who did not appeal against the decision to indict them, a decision was made on February 21, 2018, so that they were brought before the jury, when they were convicted of the crime of murder on April 13, 2018.

3.5 Lawsuit No. 0004825-18.2017.8.24.0011

In this case, the crime took place on June 29, 2017, as recorded in police report 531-2017.85. The investigation was concluded on November 9, 2017, without indictment due to the failure to identify the perpetrator.

On January 9, 2018, the Public Prosecutor's Office challenged the police chief's opinion, asking the judge to return the case file to the Judicial Police for further investigations to identify the perpetrator of the crime.

The case file is awaiting a court ruling on the request made by the Public Prosecutor's Office.

3.6 *Lawsuit No. 0003712-29.2017.8.24.0011*

In this case, the crime took place on September 8, 2017, as recorded in police report 34-2017-7047. The investigation was concluded on September 18, 2017, with three people indicted.

The Public Prosecutor's Office denounced the exact person indicted by the Police Delegate on September 26, 2017, which was received by the judge the following day.

Duly summoned, two of the defendants presented a preliminary defense by the same lawyer on October 12, 2017, in which they did not allege preliminary objections on the merits, failing to comment on the merits of the complaint at that time. A habeas corpus petition was filed to revoke the preventive detention previously ordered, and the order was denied by the Santa Catarina Court of Justice.

The third defendant presented his preliminary defense, through a judge-appointed defense attorney, who opted to comment on the merits of the complaint, without presenting any preliminary arguments.

The hearing took place on the date initially set (06/11/2017), with the Public Prosecutor's Office presenting oral closing arguments. The defense was given 3 days to present closing arguments by memorials.

On December 11, 2017, a sentence was handed down, in which the judge pronounced the Defendant, as requested in the complaint, denying them the right to appeal. A motion for clarification was filed against this judgment, which was heard and dismissed on January 15, 2018.

An appeal in the strict sense was filed against the sentence by the lawyer appointed on January 15, 2018, in which the Defendants argue for the denial of authorship, or, alternatively, for the exclusion of qualifying factors. On March 7, 2018, the appeal was received and forwarded to the Court.

On March 21, 2018, the State Attorney General's Office ruled that the appeal should be accepted and dismissed, which the court fully accepted.

Once the case was returned to the lower court, and given the resignation of the lawyers appointed by two of the defendants, who were not replaced by them, a Public Defender was appointed to continue their defense. A jury session was scheduled for September 21 of this year.

3.7 . Conclusion

From the analysis of the court cases described above, which coincide with the police inquiries that investigated the crime of homicide, opened in 2017 in the city of Brusque, some patterns can be established that will be analyzed below.

First of all, there is a certain congruence between the police chief's conclusions and the decision taken by the Public Prosecutor's Office to file the complaint. Of the six investigations, in four (66.6%) the prosecutor fully agreed with the police chief's conclusion; in only one (16.6%) did the prosecutor disagree with the conclusion that the investigation should be closed and in another (16.66%) she partially agreed with the prosecutor's conclusion, since in addition to the four accused, she denounced another person, a female.

Assertiveness of the Indictment	***Qty of Surveys***	***Percentage***
Full Concordance	4	66,6%
Partial agreement	**1**	**16,6%**
Disagreement	1	16,6%
Total	**6**	**100%**

With regard to the latter case, it should be noted that, since she died even before the summons was served, there is no way of ascertaining whether her guilt would be recognized in court.

As for the assertiveness of the indictment, the lack of a final judgment in most of the cases hampers this assessment. However, of the 11 indicted, 2 (18.1%) have already had their guilt recognized by the plenary; 1 (9.1%) has had a final judgment; 3 (27.2%) have appealed only in relation to the addition of qualifying factors in the indictment, which indicates acquiescence in the indications of authorship; 2 (18.1%) are awaiting trial in the first degree; 2 (18.1%) have filed an appeal in which they allege denial of authorship; and 1 (9.1%) has not yet presented the reasons for the appeal, thus hindering the analysis of its return effect.

Procedural Status	***Indicted***	***Percentage***
Guilt Recognized by the Plenary	3	27,2%
Innocence Recognized by the Plenary	1	9,1%
Sentence of Pronunciation Transited in Judgment	**1**	**9,1%**
Appeal against the addition of the	3	27,2%

qualifying factors		
Pending Judgment [0]	2	18,1%
Appeal based on denial of authorship	1	18,1%
Total	**11**	**100%**

At least, so far, none of the indictees have been cleared by the courts, which indicates, albeit provisionally and precariously, a good deal of assertiveness in the indictments.

As for the time taken to investigate, the fastest investigation was in the sixth case analyzed, which lasted 10 days from the date of the incident to the conclusion of the investigation, while the longest was in the fifth case, precisely the one in which the perpetrator was not found, which was reported by the police chief after 132 days since the crime occurred. On average, the investigation took 73 days.

It is clear that both the Public Prosecutor's Office and the Criminal Court act very quickly when it comes to offering and receiving complaints. Considering only the five cases in which there was a complaint, the Public Prosecutor's Office took an average of 12 days between the report of the investigation and the filing of the complaint, with the longest time being 17 days and the shortest 8 days. The Criminal Court judge, on the other hand, took an average of 5 days to receive the complaint, with the longest period being 9 days and the shortest only 1 day.

The longest time taken to resolve the cases is between the receipt of the complaint and the completion of the investigation, a result possibly influenced by the acts necessary for the summons, and their particular difficulties, as well as the deadlines for the defendants' defense. Here the average was 124 days, with the shortest period being 42 days in the last case and the longest 223 days in the third case analyzed.

With regard to the time taken to hand down the sentence, excluding the case in which it had not yet been handed down, there were 4 cases in which the average time between the end of the investigation and the sentence, including the deadline for submitting closing arguments, was 22 days, with the shortest period being 1 day and the longest 35.

Finally, taking into account the 4 cases in which there has already been a sentence, the total time between the fact and the sentence was an average of 178 days, just under 6 months, with the longest case, among those closed, lasting 222 days and the shortest, 94 days.

As for the Defendants' defenses, it can be seen that 6 presented their defense through a lawyer, while 4 presented their defense through a lawyer. One of the defendants, because she died before being summoned, did not present a defense. In addition, of the 6 who presented a defense, two had their defenses replaced by pro bono attorneys, due to the resignation of the attorneys then responsible for their defenses.

Defender costs	***Indicted***
Dative	6
Constituted	***5***
Total	11

As for the defense itself, only 2 (18.1%), represented by the same lawyer, a dativo in both cases, chose to present the defense on the merits in the response to the accusation, while the other 9 (82.8%) chose to do so in the closing arguments.

Type of Defense	***Indicted***	***Percentage***
Defense on the Merits in the Answer to the Indictment	2	18,1%
Merits in closing arguments	**9**	**82,8%**
Total	11	100%

As for the final arguments, of the 5 cases that reached this stage, only in 1 (20%) did both the prosecution and the defense present their oral arguments, in accordance with the Code of Criminal Procedure.

Means of presenting closing arguments	***Indicted***	***Percentage***
Oral	1	20%
Memorials	**4**	**80%**
Total	5	100%

It can be seen that this expedient helps to speed up judgments, since, in this case, the sentence was handed down on the day immediately following the hearing, while in the others, in one of the cases no sentence has yet been handed down (hearing held on November 29, 2017), and in the three others, the average time between hearing and sentence was 23.3 days.

4. Conclusion

It is of immense importance to build an information base with the data presented on homicide crimes, not only in Brazil, but also locally. This information, if well extracted, can be used to develop public policies aimed at reducing the staggering number of murders that occur every year in the country.[25]

It is also possible to monitor the efficiency of the Criminal Investigation Division, which is well above the national average. And, in the authors' view, there is enormous scope for public policy in the area of public security, making it possible to develop a range of preventive and repressive studies, not only by police agencies, but by the community in general, academics and organized civil society.

In the light of the data collected, the following points can be inferred, subject to interpretation and conclusions that are always subject to rectification:

- *there is no relevant data on female perpetrators of homicide (none indicted, only one reported), information that can no longer be said when analyzing the victims, considering that half of them (03) are female.*

- *no teenagers were found to be involved in any of the six murders committed in 2017, and the vast majority of those indicted are aged between 20 and 24 (70%), at the peak of their productive capacity.*

- *those involved have a low level of education, with 70% of those who have not completed secondary school, and, furthermore, none of those indicted has a university degree.*

- *04 (four) indictees, so 40% of those surveyed, have a police record for drug trafficking.*

- *the reasons given cannot be grouped together, given their lack of connection and similar causes, ranging from passion, commercial issues and drug trafficking.*

- *Most of the victims were born in Brusque, were killed in the same neighborhoods where they lived, had low levels of education and were equally divided between men (03) and women (03).*

- *in relation to the circumstances of the crimes, it is worth noting that, although the characteristics of each homicide have been investigated, at least in 2017, they occurred for*

---

25 http://agenciabrasil.ebc.com.br/geral/noticia/2017-10/com-mais-de-61-mil-assassinatos-brasil-tem-record-homicides-in-2016

different reasons and in a non-linear way.

- *the linear fact that approximately 70% of homicides were committed with firearms (02 revolvers, 01 pistol and 01 handmade weapon) stands out.*

Having made these conclusions, it is important to emphasize the need to develop other similar studies, restricted territorially, considering the immensity of production at national level, but the regional scarcity, in order to be able to compare, examine and reflect the local criminal situation.

According to widespread media coverage and statistical support, there is currently an epidemic of homicides in Brazil, a nonsense that affects young people with low levels of education, who are poor and are usually killed by firearms, data that largely coincides with that collected here.

In order to change this scenario, in addition to the necessary public education and employment policies, including the valorization of police officers, we need the operators of the justice system (security agents or not) to consolidate the idea of efficiency and transparency, publishing their results and showing their costs.

In doing so, they will enhance the legitimacy of their hard work while providing their managers with the means to make better decisions.

And on this last point, we believe we have made a small contribution.

Special thanks:

We would like to thank Civil Police Officer Pedro Henrique Lussolli for his help, both in providing and collecting the data, without which the research would have been slower and less effective. At the same time, we congratulate all the civil police officers in the region, who maintained a high level of resolution of homicide crimes committed in the city of Brusque during the year under review.

Bibliographical references

BISPO, Fàbio. **Florianópolis closes 2017 with historic record for violent deaths.** Available at: <https://ndonline.com.br/florianopolis/noticias/florianopolis- closes-2017-with-historic-record-of-violent-deaths> Accessed on April 10, 2018.

CALHAU, Lélio Braga. **Social control - Informal and Formal.** Available at:http://clodomiro.xpg.uol.com.br/e724.html. Accessed on: Aug. 11, 2016.

2010 IBGE CENSUS. Available at:

https://censo2010.ibge.gov.br/sinopse/index.php?dados=26&uf=42> Accessed April 10, 2018

DUARTE, Alessandra. **IBGE data confirms that violence kills more young men**. Available at: <https://oglobo.globo.com/brasil/dados-do-ibge- confirm-that-violence-kills-more-young-men-3256278> Accessed on April 10, 2018

HAMADA, Fernando Massami; Do Amaral, José Hamilton**. Criminal profiling as a criminological tool - encontro de iniciaçâo cientifica**. Vol. 4, 2009.

INFOPEN, **Levantamento nacional de informaçôes Penitenciarias**, year 5, 2014. Available at: <http://dados.gov.br/dataset/infopen-levantamento-nacional-de- informacoes-penitenciarias> Accessed on: July 27, 2016.

LISBOA, Vinicius. **Seven out of ten homicides in Brazil in 2015 were with firearms**. Available at: http://agenciabrasil.ebc.com.br/geral/noticia/2017- 06/seven-out-of-ten-homicides-in-brazil-were-firearms-in-2015 Accessed April 10, 2018

MELLO, Daniel. **With more than 61,000 murders, Brazil has a record number of homicides in 2016.** Available at:

<http://agenciabrasil.ebc.com.br/geral/noticia/2017-10/com-mais-de-61-mil- murders-brazil-have-record-homicides-in-2016> Accessed April 10, 2018

ITAJÂI VALLEY MESOREGION. Available at: <https://pt.wikipedia.org/wiki/Mesorregi%C3%A3o_do_Vale_do_Itaja%C3%AD> Accessed on April 10, 2018 OLIVEIRA, Rafael Niebuhr Maia de; MARCOLLA, Fernanda Analu. Comparative analysis of the criminological profile of the Brusque prison population in relation to the national average: evidence of the selectivity of the Brazilian punitive system. In: OLDONI, Fabiano; SILVA, Pollyana Maria da (Orgs.). **Study on the prison system:** from selectivity to illegality. Joinville: Manuscritos Editora, 2017. p. 81104.

PAULA, Tania Braga de. **Criminology: study of the sociological schools of crime and the practice of criminal offenses**. 2013. 47 f. Monograph (Graduation in Law) - Centro Universitàrio do Norte Paulista - UNORP, Sao José do Rio Preto, 2013.

ROBERGE, Joao Vitor. **Brusque records highest number of homicides in three years in 2017**. Available at: https://omunicipio.com.br/brusque-teve-seis- homicides-in-2017-highest-ever-recorded-since-2014/ Accessed on April 10, 2018.

SALVAGNI, Anelize. 2010 Census: **Santa Catarina has 500,000 more women than men**. Available at: <http://dc.clicrbs.com.br/sc/noticia/2011/11/censo- 2010-santa-catarina-has-500-mil-women-more-than-men-3562973.html> Accessed April 10, 2018

SANTA CATARINA. Court of Justice. **Criminal Action n. 0001239-70.2017.8.24.0011.**

Available at:

https://esaj.tjsc.jus.br/cpopg/show.do?processo.codigo=0B0051CR40000&processo.foro=11 &uuidCaptcha=sajcaptcha_0827ef7e065d48ceb8065588c58e17d9. Accessed on September 10, 2018.

SANTA CATARINA. Court of Justice. **Criminal Action n.** ***000395218.2017.8.24.0011.*** Available at:

https://esaj.tjsc.jus.br/cpopg/show.do?processo.codigo=0B005100D0000&processo.foro=11&uuidCaptcha=sajcaptcha_e57680eaf74c46968293dfd89c4ff954 . Accessed on: September 10, 2018.

SANTA CATARINA. Court of Justice. **Criminal Action n. 0002182-87.2017.8.24.0011.**

Available at:

https://esaj.tjsc.jus.br/cpopg/show.do?processo.codigo=0B0051GCR0000&processo.foro=11&uuidCaptcha=sajcaptcha_3d75b8cc6f6043b6a1b054e8cd470127 . Accessed on: Sep. 10, 2018

SANTA CATARINA. Court of Justice. **Criminal Action n. 0000845-29.2018.8.24.0011**

Available at:

https://esaj.tjsc.jus.br/cpopg/show.do?processo.codigo=0B0051XLA0000&processo.foro=11&uuidCaptcha=sajcaptcha_dcf0ac18d2524e0f928e13a3cf7c0865 . Accessed on: Sep. 10, 2018

SANTA CATARINA. Court of Justice. **Criminal Action n. 0004825-18.2017.8.24.0011**

Available at:

https://esaj.tjsc.jus.br/cpopg/show.do?processo.codigo=0B0051S5S0000&processo.foro=11&uuidCaptcha=sajcaptcha 5742f4c222f84e8f94988531 c1e49355 .

Accessed on: September 10, 2018

SANTA CATARINA. Court of Justice. **Criminal Action n. 0004825-18.2017.8.24.0011**

Available at:

https://esaj.tjsc.jus.br/cpopg/show.do?processo.codigo=0B0051S5S0000&processo.foro=11&uuidCaptcha=sajcaptcha 5742f4c222f84e8f94988531c1e49355 .

Accessed on: September 10, 2018

SARAIVA, Adriana. **Population reaches 205.5 million, with fewer whites and more browns and blacks.** Available at <https://agenciadenoticias.ibge.gov.br/agencia-noticias/2012-agencia-de-noticias/noticias/18282-pnad-c-moradores.html> Accessed on April 10, 2018.

Printed by Books on Demand GmbH, Norderstedt / Germany